BigTime® Piano

Christmas

Level 4
Intermediate

This book belongs to: _____

Arranged by

Nancy and Randall Faber

Production Coordinator: Jon Ophoff
Design and Illustration: Terpstra Design, San Francisco
Engraving: Dovetree Productions, Inc.

FABER
PIANO ADVENTURES®

3042 Creek Drive
Ann Arbor, Michigan 48108

A NOTE TO TEACHERS

BigTime® Piano Christmas is an entertaining and educational collection of Christmas favorites arranged for the intermediate pianist. Both traditional and popular Christmas favorites are included. The arrangements offer a variety of sounds and styles, always capturing the spirit of Christmas.

BigTime® Piano Christmas is part of the *BigTime® Piano* series. "BigTime" designates Level 4 of the *PreTime® to BigTime® Piano Supplementary Library* arranged by Faber and Faber.

Following are the levels of the supplementary library, which lead from *PreTime®* to *BigTime®*.

PreTime® Piano	(Primer Level)
PlayTime® Piano	(Level 1)
ShowTime® Piano	(Level 2A)
ChordTime® Piano	(Level 2B)
FunTime® Piano	(Level 3A–3B)
BigTime® Piano	(Level 4)

Each level offers books in a variety of styles, making it possible for the teacher to offer stimulating material for every student. For a complimentary detailed listing, e-mail faber@pianoadventures.com or write us at the mailing address below.

Visit **www.PianoAdventures.com**.

Helpful Hints:

1. Hands-alone practice can be very helpful when learning a piece.

2. The songs can be assigned in any order. It is often best to allow the student's interest and enthusiasm to determine the order of selection.

3. Teachers and students will find these arrangements to be delightful for Christmas recitals, church programs or other seasonal events.

ISBN 978-1-61677-016-7

TABLE OF CONTENTS

The First Noel

TRADITIONAL

Moderately

The___ first_____ No - el, the___ an - gel did say, was to cer - tain poor shep - herds in fields as they lay. In___ fields_____ where___ they lay___ keep - ing their sheep, on a

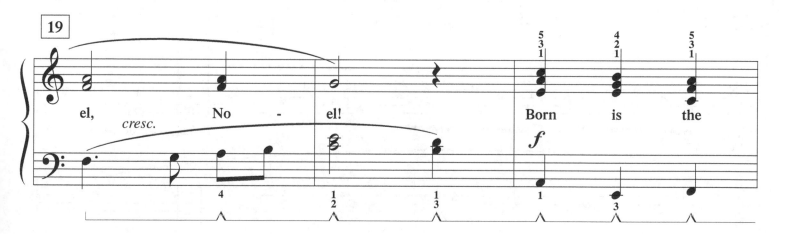

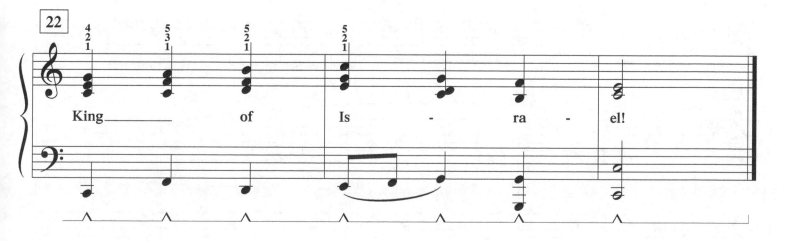

What Child Is This?

A TRADITIONAL ENGLISH TUNE

A Holly Jolly Christmas

Music and Lyrics by
JOHNNY MARKS

Brightly, with swing

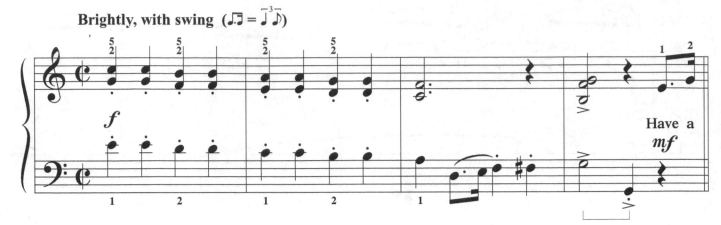

Hol - ly Jol - ly Christ - mas, it's the best time of the year.
Hol - ly Jol - ly Christ - mas, and when you walk down the street,

I don't know if there'll be snow, but have a cup of
say hel - lo to friends you know and

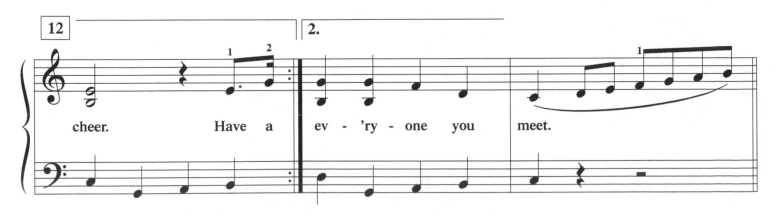

cheer. Have a
ev - 'ry - one you meet.

It Came Upon the Midnight Clear

By E. H. SEARS and
R. S. WILLIS

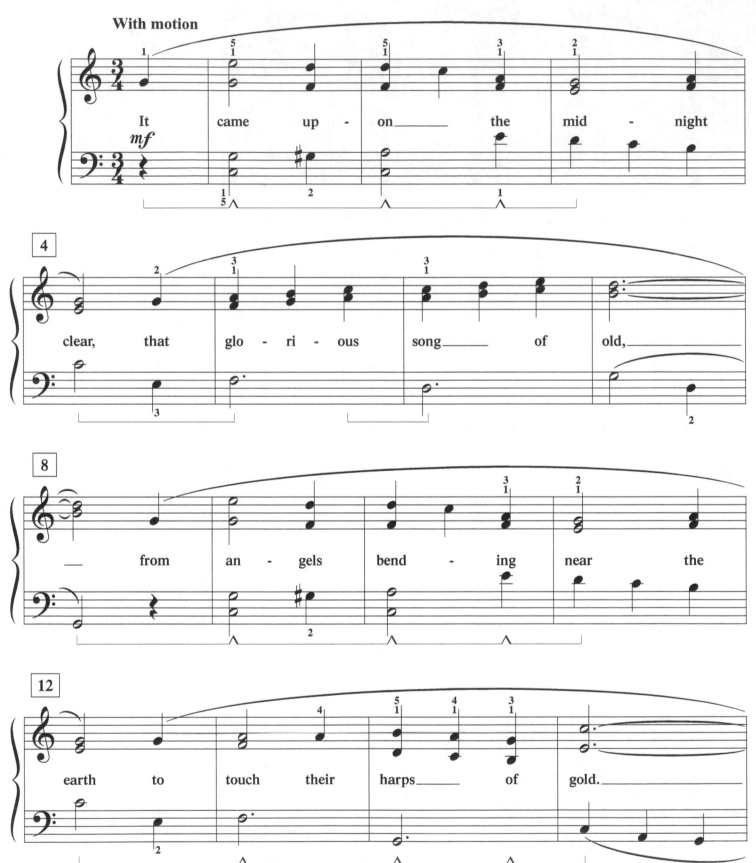

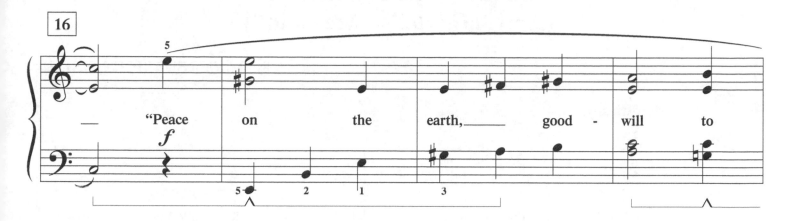

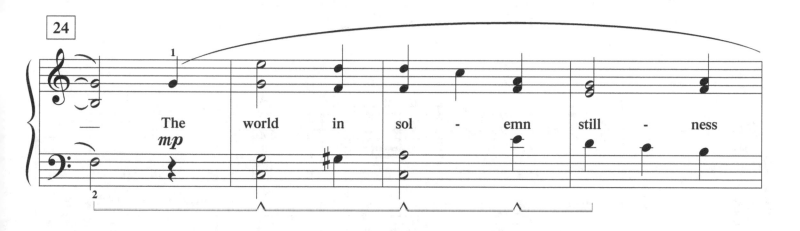

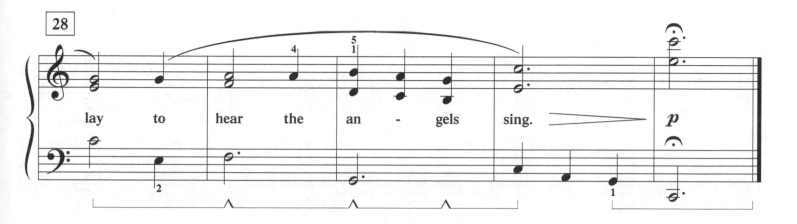

Hallelujah Chorus
(from Handel's "Messiah")

By GEORGE FREDERICK HANDEL

Majestically

Hal - le - lu - jah! Hal - le - lu - jah! Hal - le -

lu - jah! Hal - le - lu - jah! Hal - le - lu - jah! Hal - le - lu - jah!

Hal - le - lu - jah! Hal - le - lu - jah! Hal - le - lu - jah! Hal - le - lu - jah!

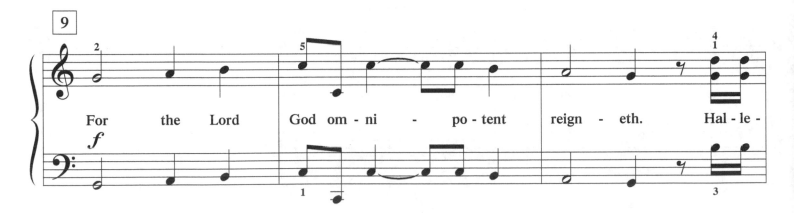

For the Lord God om - ni - po - tent reign - eth. Hal - le -

12 lu - jah! Hal - le - lu - jah! Hal - le - lu - jah! Hal - le - lu - jah! For the Lord

15 God om - ni - po - tent reign - eth; *mf* And He shall

And He shall reign...

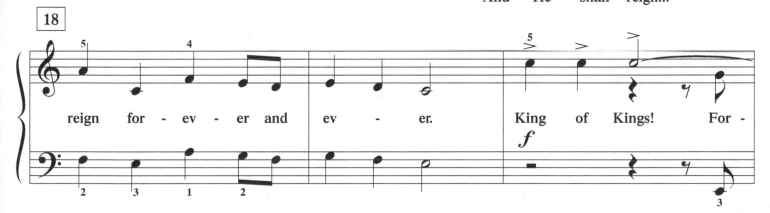

18 reign for - ev - er and ev - er. King of Kings! For -

21 ev - er and ev - er, and Lord of Lords! Hal - le - lu - jah! Hal - le - lu - jah! Hal - le -

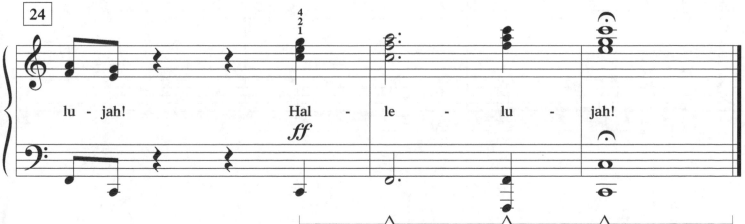

24 lu - jah! Hal - le - lu - jah!

Silent Night

Music by FRANZ GRÜBER
Words by JOSEPH MOHR

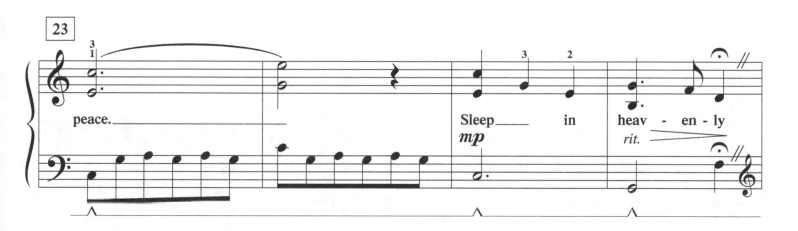

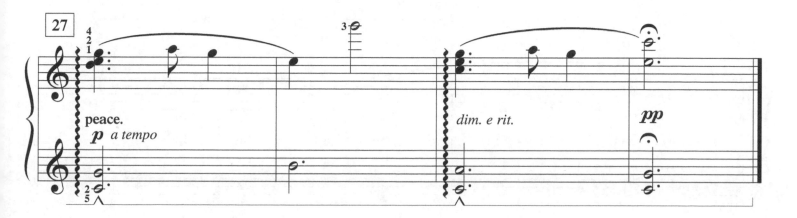

Hark! The Herald Angels Sing

By FELIX MENDELSSOHN and
CHAS. WESLEY

Joyously

mf

Hark! the her - ald an - gels sing,___ "Glo - ry to the

new - born King! Peace on earth and mer - cy mild,___

God and sin - ners re - con - ciled." Joy - ful, all ye

na - tions rise,____ join the tri - umph of the skies.____

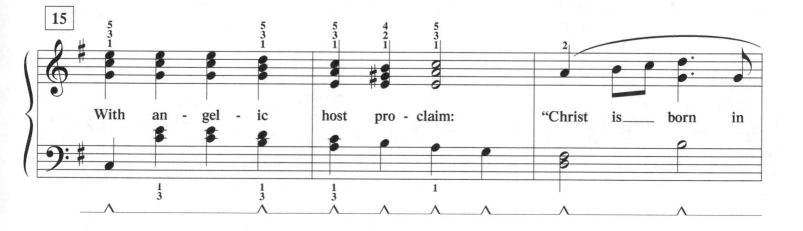

With an - gel - ic host pro - claim: "Christ is____ born in

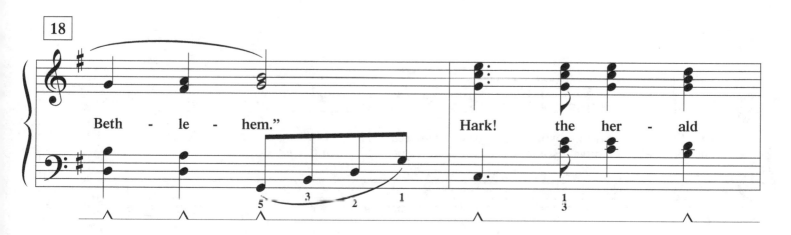

Beth - le - hem." Hark! the her - ald

an - gels sing, "Glo - ry____ to the new - born King!"

rit.

Rockin' Around the Christmas Tree

Music and Lyrics by
JOHNNY MARKS

Let It Snow! Let It Snow! Let It Snow!

Lyric by
SAMMY CAHN

Music by
JULE STYNE

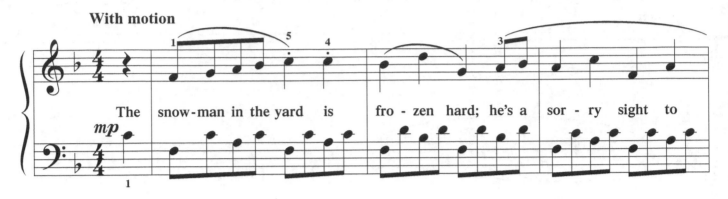

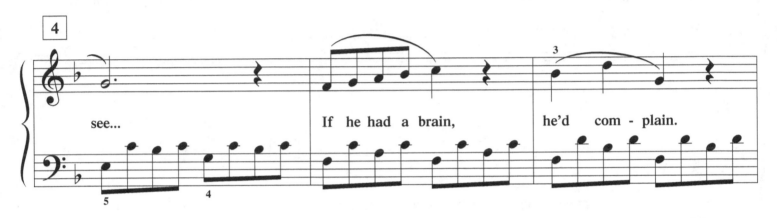

since we've no place to go, Let it snow! Let it snow! Let it

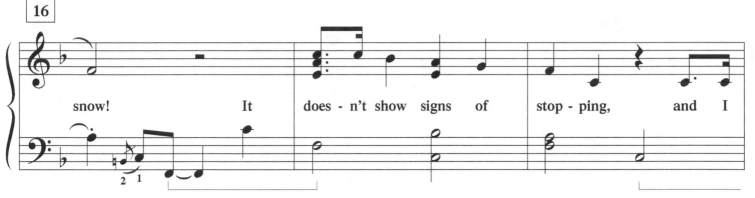

snow! It does-n't show signs of stop-ping, and I

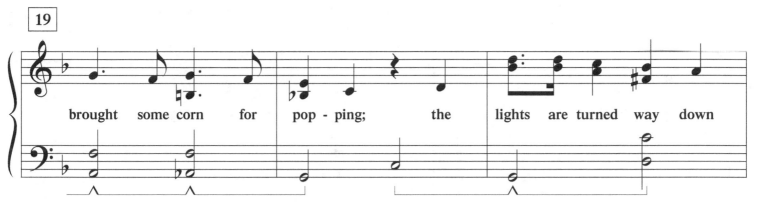

brought some corn for pop-ping; the lights are turned way down

low, Let it snow! Let it snow! Let it snow! When we

mp

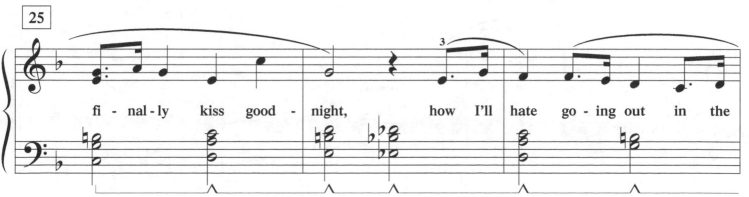

fi-nal-ly kiss good-night, how I'll hate go-ing out in the

storm! But as long as you hold me tight, *cresc.*

all the way home I'll be warm. The fire___ is slow-ly

dy-ing and my dear, we're still good-bye-ing, but as

long as you love me so, Let it snow! Let it

snow! Let it snow! Let it snow! Let it snow!

Carol of the Bells

Words by
PETER J. WILHOUSKY

Music by
M. LEONTOVICH

FF1016

24

17

Ding, dong, ding, dong, that is their song, with joy-ful ring all car-ol-ing.

21

One seems to hear words of good cheer from ev-'ry-where, fill-ing the air.

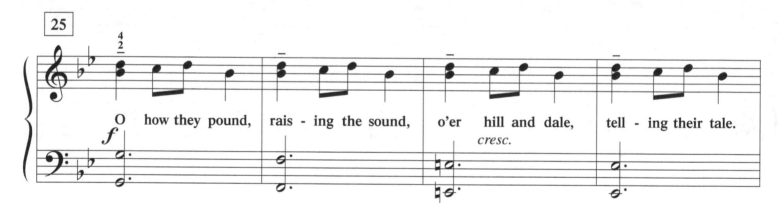

25

O how they pound, rais-ing the sound, o'er hill and dale, tell-ing their tale.

29

Gai - ly they ring___ while peo-ple sing___ songs of good cheer,___

32

Christ - mas is here! Mer - ry, mer - ry, mer - ry, mer - ry Christ - mas!

35

Mer - ry, mer - ry, mer - ry, mer - ry Christ - mas! On, on they send,

38

on with - out end, their joy - ful tone to ev - 'ry home. On, on they send,

42

on with - out end, their joy - ful tone to ev - 'ry home.

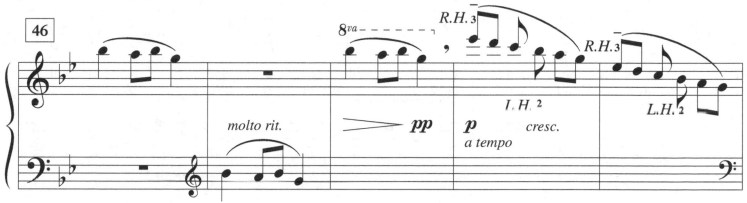

46

51

Slowly

Ding, dong, ding, dong.

I Heard the Bells on Christmas Day

Music by JOHNNY MARKS
Lyrics by HENRY WADSWORTH LONGFELLOW
Adapted by JOHNNY MARKS

Jesu, Joy of Man's Desiring

J.S. BACH

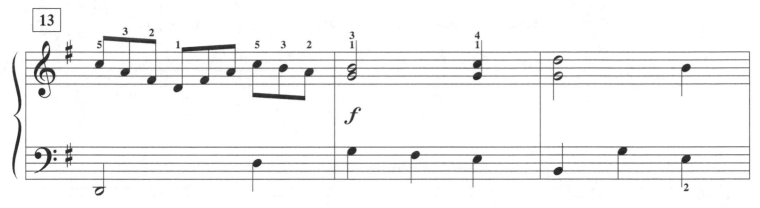

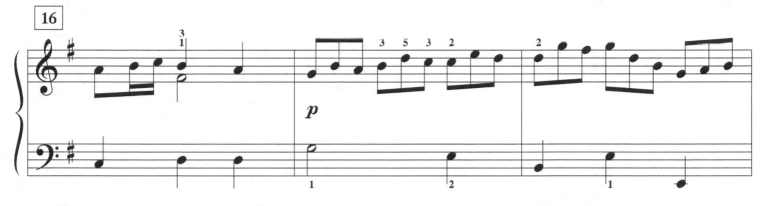

O Come, O Come, Emmanuel

English Lyric by
JOHN M. NEALE

Music Adapted by
THOMAS HELMORE

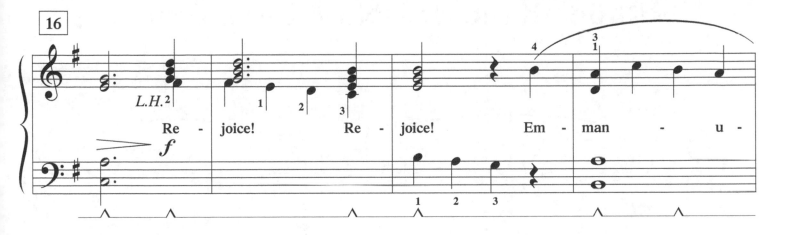

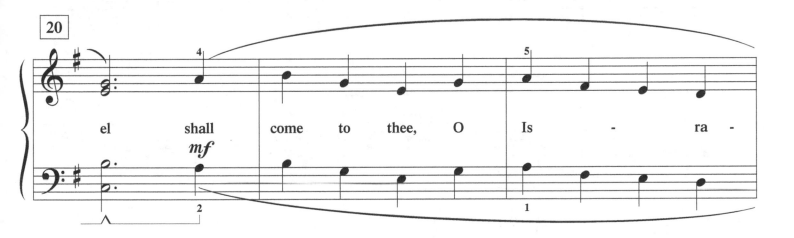

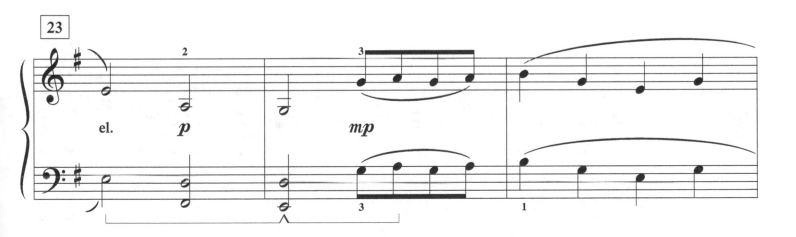

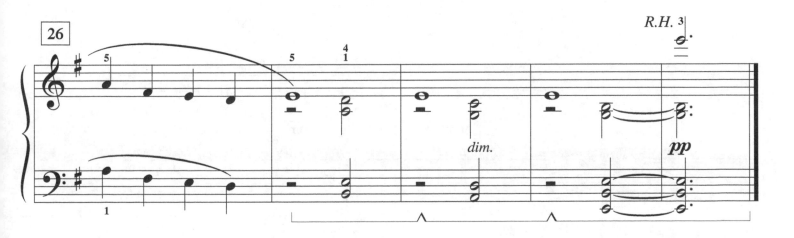

Rudolph the Red-Nosed Reindeer

Music and Lyrics by
JOHNNY MARKS

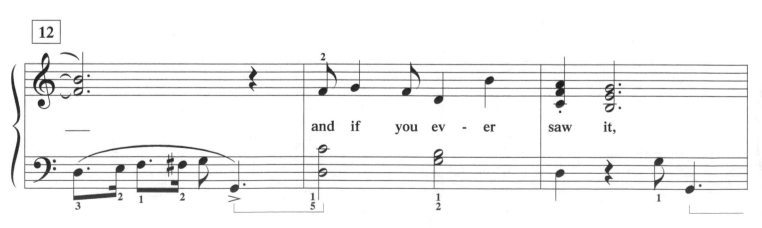

Then how the rein-deer loved him as they shout-ed out with glee,

"Ru-dolph, the red-nosed rein-deer,

you'll go down in his-to-ry!"

Winter Wonderland

Words by
DICK SMITH

Music by
FELIX BERNARD

FF1016

O Holy Night

By ADOLPH ADAM

Moderato

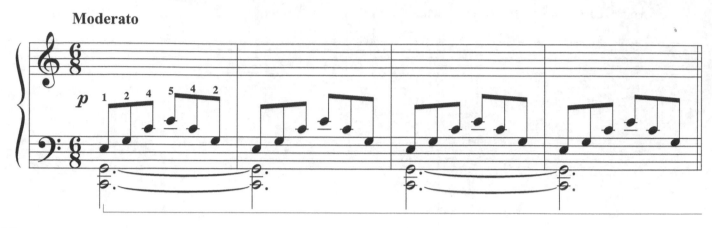

O ho - ly night!____ The stars are bright - ly shin -

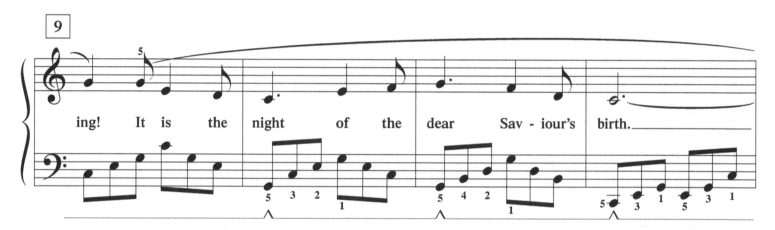

ing! It is the night of the dear Sav - iour's birth.____

Long lay the world____ in sin and sor - row